JUMPING HURDLES
Devotional Moments for Overcoming in the Quiet of the Storm

Π

Dr. Latisha D. Reeves-Henry

JUMPING HURDLES
Devotional Moments for Overcoming in the Quiet of the Storm

Copyright © 2023 by Latisha D. Reeves-Henry

All rights reserved. No portion of this publication may be reproduced, distributed, or transmitted in any form or by any means, including photocopying, recording, or other electronic or mechanical methods, without the prior written permission of the publisher, except in the case of brief quotations embodied in critical reviews and certain other noncommercial uses permitted by copyright law.

For permission requests, write to the publisher addressed "ATTN: Permissions" at the following:

Sh'Shares NETWORK, LLC, PO BOX 13202, Jacksonville, FL 32206

Discounts are available on bulk orders by associations and corporations for business, educational, and ministry use. For details, contact the publisher at the address above.

ISBN: 978-1-942650-59-1

Printed in the United States of America
First Edition

Scripture taken from the New King James Version®. Copyright © 1982 by Thomas Nelson. Used by permission. All rights reserved.

Scripture taken from the New King James Version®. Copyright © 1982 by Thomas Nelson. Used by permission. All rights reserved.

Scripture quotations marked HCSB are taken from the Holman Christian Standard Bible®, Used by Permission HCSB ©1999,2000,2002,2003,2009 Holman Bible Publishers. Holman Christian Standard Bible®, Holman CSB®, and HCSB® are federally registered trademarks of Holman Bible Publishers.

*To the One who works all things together
and loves me without reservation,
my yes is perpetual because Your loving kindness is eternal.
Thank You, God, Faithful Lover of My Soul, forever.*

Π

*To my tribe,
Thank you.
That you encourage me and never let me settle does not go
unnoticed. I appreciate each of you.*

Contents

Contents v
Introduction vii

JUMPING HURDLES 1

When All of That Still Ain't Enough 3
Lord! Ain't Nobody Else in The Room 5
He Will Do It! 9
Sometimes, It's Better to Just Be Quiet! 13
I Am in God's Hands 17
"NO" is Good, Too 19
The Scent of a Woman 21
Putty In God's Hands 25
We Glory in God!!!   *(Foolishness and All)* 29
The Power of Peace: On Guard 31
Call Him 35
You Will Know 37
In Everything?? 39
He is Still Doing It 43
Give Them What You've Got 45
What Does Jesus Do? 47
I Wanna Be Yours 51
What's the Goal? 55
What If God Doesn't and You Don't 59
Yes, God Can Use You 63
Increase Anyway 65
Qualified by God 67
Joy Will Come 71
Life Lessons from a Dark Place 73
God of the Victory 77
Rest in His Love 81
Chart the Course 83
Gratefulness 85
It Shall Come Forth 87
Christ's Love Speaks Through Our Lives 89
Come Out 91
    About the Author 94
    Connect 94

Introduction

Recent years have been particularly trying. Like many, I have had to navigate everything from personal failure to the rigors of ministry challenges and the unexpected deaths of beloved family, friends, and mentors, all in rapid succession. I hate Covid, cancer, and heart disease! Throw in a horrific, debilitating accident that nearly cost my husband his life and drastically altered our livelihood and manner of being. The aftermath of this traumatic incident cast shadows of situational depression over our lives. Everything looked different: prayer, praise, weeping, wailing, reading, studying. Still, I couldn't breathe. My thoughts were cloudy. I knew I wasn't alone, but I couldn't feel. I had endured storms and crises before, but this season was vastly different. Therein, you have the title and making of the message in this book.

Several years ago, I learned that the lightning of a storm coupled with the gases in the air has the same effect fertilizer has on the grass, trees, plants, and foliage. Thunderstorms can produce exponential growth in the right atmospheric conditions. If we allow it to be, the same exponential growth is possible in the thunderstorms of our lives as well.

I don't particularly care for, nor do I seek out, the storms of life. Still, I admit that a new level of spiritual maturing helped me appreciate the value of the storms and respect their power and role in transforming my perspective and honoring God's sovereignty.

In the center of the storm is where I am learning to lean in so that I can dwell more deeply under the shadow of God's wings, cherish the place of refuge, and abide there—where there is clarity, safety, and shelter. There, is where I learn to overcome, love, live, thrive, and give my life away so that I may live abundantly. Under the safety of God's wing is where I learn how to go with the direction of the Wind instead of struggling against Him. With God's protection, I learned to find my pace and hit my stride. Ultimately, God helps me run the race and clear the hurdles to overcome.

I pray that the words in this devotional bring peace, strength, and comfort to all who read them. Keep jumping hurdles because there is always something to overcome, but let us learn to embrace the wisdom we gain from the lessons of the storms.

Sincerely,
Latisha

JUMPING
HURDLES
Π

When All of That Still Ain't Enough

PSALM 42:1-4 NKJV
*As the deer pants for the water brooks,
So pants my soul for You, O God.
My soul thirsts for God, for the Living God.
When shall I come and appear before God?
My tears have been my food day and night. While
they continually say to me, "Where is your God?"
When I remember these things, I pour out my soul
within me. For I used to go with the multitude;
I went with them to the house of God,
with the voice of joy and praise,
with a multitude that kept a pilgrim feast.*

This particular Psalm is one of my favorites. I can visualize the deer with an overwhelming innate desire to consume the life-giving source. It's a beautiful picture! What happens to me, then, when I am panting?

I once found myself in this same state of longing for Living Water, but I didn't understand it. I was "in church" every week. I was in the sanctuary for devotion and Sunday morning services at 8:00 a.m. and 11:00 a.m. I attended Wednesday night Bible study, Sunday School, and even small group sessions. I passed out tracts, served the sick and poor, and visited those in prison and

Dr. Latisha D. Henry-Reeves

anywhere else that was needed. I even went to different small groups that weren't my own. I was *doing* and *going* to the point of exhaustion. Still, I found myself longing while asking, "God, where are You? Don't You see me doing all of this??

Unfortunately, if we are honest, there is no way around it; often, this level of church attendance, service, and participation is what we are taught to do. Our mentors and leaders even promote this rigorous cycle as fulfillment, proof of allegiance, and sincere faith.

When I eventually found myself living in drought while serving amongst people who had the river of life flowing within them, God led me to this Psalm. I realized there was a longing and thirst that could be quenched only by sitting in God's presence and allowing God's peace to calm me. Perhaps you can relate to this intense desire to be close to the One who loves us with reckless abandon and makes us smile, laugh, and dance with exuberant joy — even in times of distress. That form of peace does not come from *doing* and *going*.

As I pondered the contemplative words of this psalmist, I applied them to our modern-day context. It was then that I concluded that my longing for gathering stemmed from a desire to gather with persons of like mind and heart. At its core, it was about offering the sacrifice of praise and authentic worship in God's presence, where there is safety and fullness of joy. I stopped doing and stopped going so I could try to find relief. I began sitting and listening, praying and journaling, reading and thinking, sometimes crying and asking questions. I did all of this with God as my audience. Near immediately, my soul was no longer cast down. Finally, I had re-discovered rest and encouraged myself to hope in God and yet praise the help of my countenance.

PRAYER:

Lord God, thank You for the call to authentic relationship and worship that allows us to exalt You above every circumstance. Help us surrender and stop trying to prove worth for acceptance. Let us declare Your goodness no matter the season.

Lord! Ain't Nobody Else in The Room

Hosea 2:19-20 NKJV
I will betroth you to Me forever;
Yes, I will betroth you to Me in righteousness.
and justice, lovingkindness and mercy.
I will betroth you to Me in faithfulness,
and you shall know the Lord.

It's funny how we grow up having certain expectations of one another and God. Babies expect to be nurtured, fed, changed, rocked, and cared for regardless of whether it's day or night; they have those piercing screams to prove it. Toddlers expect every living and moving thing to bow to their whimsical view of the whole wide world, which they view as a playground to explore.

Each family also has expectations. While growing up, my mother always expected my brother to fight on my behalf, and so did I. Since I would get up and get dressed early, I was expected to help make sure my brother got up and off to school with me, on time. That made no sense to me because he was older, but I guess that's the price of having a bodyguard, and those were the expectations. This snapshot view of my family is just one picture of how expectations are so much a part of our lives from our earliest understanding.

Old and New Testament records provide quite the story of various people who were often distracted by their desires. They were deeply disappointed when God failed to meet their "people-imposed" expectations. The Bible is loaded with stories sharing the consequences of people who stumbled, forgot, or sinned because God's plan did not line up with what they expected in the way they expected it. The chronicles of our lives are read in much the same way.

My plan at age 20 was to be married and career-oriented by age 25. That didn't happen. At 29, I planned to have a master's degree, a husband, and financial stability by age 35. My plan changed yet again at 35. By age 40, I would be married with that master's degree in hand and operating in ministry. Unfortunately, in my misguided years, I tried many times to ensure that marriage would come. Marriage seemed to not come on my schedule, no matter what I tried. There were many disappointments and self-imposed consequences as a result. My life was a mess. I looked around one day, and *still*, there was nobody else in the room. It eventually dawned on me that my heart and my life belonged to God to shape.

At age 53, I read Hosea 2:19-20 with the degrees and now the husband. I have served in various locations in ministry and non-profit organizations for 26 years and counting. I am reminded that God's desire for our lives, our hopes, and our dreams will be found in God's will; our expectations will not govern them. In the Bible, we repeatedly see how God's people are promised restoration after their failures. God promised to have mercy upon them and to unite with them. God wanted them to honor the covenant relationship and let their expectations be for God's faithfulness. God wants the same of you and me, even if nobody else is in the room.

PRAYER:

> God, we are grateful that
> You are always in the room.
> That's what matters most because we have
> everything we need since You are there.
> You are the source and the supply.
> We are never alone in You.

He Will Do It!

PSALM 37:1-9, 16-18, 23 NKJV

Do not fret because of evildoers, nor be envious of the workers of iniquity. For they shall soon be cut down like the grass and wither as the green herb. Trust in the Lord and do good; dwell in the land and feed on His faithfulness. Delight yourself in the Lord and He shall give you the desires of your heart. Commit your way to the Lord, trust also in Him, and He shall bring it to pass. He shall bring forth your righteousness as the light and your justice as the noonday. Rest in the Lord and wait patiently for Him; do not fret because of him who prospers in his way, because of the man who brings wicked schemes to pass. Cease from anger and forsake wrath; do not fret--it only causes harm. For evildoers shall be cut off, but those who wait on the Lord they shall inherit the earth.

A little that the righteous man has is better than the riches of many wicked. For the arms of the wicked shall be broken but the Lord upholds the righteous. The Lord knows the days of the upright and their inheritance shall be forever. The steps of a good man are ordered by the Lord and He delights in his way.

Dr. Latisha D. Henry-Reeves

Psalm 37 is a personal favorite. I mean, who can't relate to it? How often do we look around in frustration at the vast disparity of life? The rich get richer, and the poor get poorer. Power brokers are often so far removed from the lives of everyday hardworking people that empathy, justice, equity, and compassion for all people do not even appear to factor in policy decisions. It can feel like liberty and justice are not for all, unless your income or status dictates that you are deserving. The health and well-being of all citizens are not a genuine concern for many. This Psalm further proves there is nothing new under the sun. Wickedness becomes more sophisticated in its appearance, but evil is still what it is. That is why Psalm 37 is so important.

This Psalm, which is attributed to David, is centuries-old wisdom, a poetic song. A few of the things we can learn from this Psalm are:

- We must trust in the Lord while we do good and rely, depend, and feed on His faithfulness. Trusting God, and waiting on Him, does not equate to being idle. We must continue to do good and stand for what is right without compromising.
- We must commit our ways, plans, and desires to the Lord and submit to His authority and authorship. As we do that in our intimate relationship with Him, our desires for ourselves and humanity will align with His. That's an act of submission of one's will, and the result is that the desires of one's heart begin to align with God's desires.
- We should not spend our time consumed with the ways of the wicked. Being passionate about advocating for justice is decidedly different from being consumed with the ways of the wicked. Justice makes life better, while consumption

makes us bitter and causes us harm. The wicked gon' be wicked! We must challenge and advocate, knowing that God handles their consequences. Bitter vengeance destroys.

II. We must remember that our steps have been ordered and trust that God is who God says He is. We state that God is always good, yet we must believe it when we say it. Daily, we embrace that our path and steps have purpose and that God is weaving a beautiful tapestry that we cannot see. This faith is not optional—it's a must!

This Psalm 37 approach to life does not make me weak. It makes me stronger for longer. This approach does not render me voiceless. It makes the call clearer and the tone of clarity more powerful. It does not make me idle, passive, or lazy but fuels my fire and guards my time to make my work more fruitful.

Prayer:

Father, direct our thoughts and order our steps.
Give us wisdom and fresh ideas.
Let our actions be fueled by your love
and not by bitterness.
Keep us from focusing on what we do not have.
Keep us from forgetting what we do have.
Please help us to use what we have in order
to stand, fight, and give voice to what is right
according to your will.
You have not forgotten us.
You will bring it to pass.

Sometimes, It's Better to Just Be Quiet!

PSALM 3:3-5 HCSB
> But You, Lord, are a shield around me, my glory, and the One who lifts up my head. I cry aloud to the Lord, and He answers me from His holy mountain. I lie down and sleep; I wake again because the Lord sustains me.

PSALM 4:8 HCSB
> I will both lie down and sleep in peace, for You alone, Lord, make me live in safety.

Have you ever been troubled but couldn't put your finger on the reason why? Have you ever had so many thoughts, desires, and ideas racing through your mind about what you have to do the next day or the next few days that you could not even rest at the end of the day? Has a storm ever lasted in your life longer than two days? What about your friends or family? Are they consumed by the complexities of their not-easily-resolved issues while waiting to catch up with God's declaration over their lives? These are situations where the NOW isn't matching the WILL BE, and the imagination is working overtime—sometimes agreeing with the foolish babble of the enemy.

That is precisely why I am glad that God knows my goings and comings and every step I will take. That means God not only knows the way that I will take, but God also knows every obstacle along the path. He is fully aware of every danger and demonic force that seeks to thwart the plan and every distraction that I willingly entertain or fall prey to unknowingly.

Sometimes, the distractions of life can leave us with a heaviness and weariness that causes us to lower the shield of faith and forget to wield the sword. We are then vulnerable to the snare of the enemy. We begin to anxiously ponder, declare, and subsequently *change* over and over what God has said, may not have said, could have done, should have done, is doing, or should be doing until we are thoroughly confused and exhausted. If that is not enough, we then fall prey to doubt and unbelief because our focus becomes our fear, pain point, and then our confession.

What follows next?

Spiraling.

"After all that, now I *really* can't recall what God said!"

I thank God that He lifts our bowed heads as He surrounds us and gives us peace amid every storm…

…IF we would just let Him.

I've learned that, in these times, it is better *not* to speak unless I choose to speak life. Many are the afflictions of the righteous, but the Lord delivers us from them all. We are safest in Him. He surrounds us. He gives peace and sweet rest and lets us go to sleep.

Sit with God in honest confession and let Him quiet those thoughts. SHHHHHHH…

When I stopped rehearsing the sound of my complaints to others, I heard the sound of God's voice quieting the anguish within, lifting my bowed head and replenishing my soul.

PRAYER:

**Lord Jesus, I thank You that we find rest in You
because there is peace in You.
Thank You for being our glory
and the lifter of our heads**

I Am in God's Hands

ISAIAH 49:16 NKJV
*See, I have inscribed you
on the palms of My hands;
Your walls are continually before Me.*

The book of Isaiah often speaks of the coming of the Servant Savior we know as Christ. I am always overwhelmed by the authority and accuracy of the voice of the true biblical prophets. Clearly, it is because the words they spoke were given by God—words that were fulfilled and are still being fulfilled to this day. These prophets of old were not fueled by the American dream. There was no fluff, no self-seeking appeal to placate the greed, pride, and false hopes of the vulnerable or disobedient who go their own way. With these true prophets, the word was just plain ole' truth. Of course, judgment followed the stiff-necked, but restoration was a central theme spoken by God through the prophets as well. Now, I can rejoice and say, THANK GOD FOR HOPE!!

The forty-ninth chapter of Isaiah contains part of the oracles of salvation. At the time it was written, this chapter of Isaiah spoke directly to God's chosen people—

to those exiled. It now speaks to Jew and Gentile alike — to all who have ears to hear.

For all who are in relationship with Him, I love how God reminds us that He WILL NOT FORGET! It helps us to understand that although there are seasons when we must endure trouble, trial, and hardship — sometimes by our own hand — GOD DOES NOT FORGET US OR NEGLECT US.

Yes, God was speaking specifically to the exiles in their circumstances, but this message also rings valid for His children today. Be encouraged! A woman cannot forget the fragile, helpless, dependent child who is nursing at her bosom, but — even if she does — the word says God will not — God *cannot* — forget us. It is not in God's nature, His essence, or His character to neglect His children.

Verse sixteen says, "See I have inscribed you on the palms of My hands; Your walls are continually before me." That means I am always on God's mind, always in God's hands. It implies that there can be no separation. *Inscribed* means to be engraved so no one can erase it!

No distance will cause God not to see me, even when I can't see Him or myself! It reminds me that nothing can separate me from God's love.[1] But God doesn't even stop there. God says, "Your walls are continually before Me." God is concerned about our well-being consistently — yes, constantly and forever.[2]

God sees. God knows. God cares.

PRAYER:

**God, I thank you.
We are in Your hands and on your mind.
ALWAYS.**

---

[1] Romans 8:38-39
[2] Psalm 40:5

"NO" is Good, Too

"NO!"

It's good, too! Remember that!

The basis for the NO I am talking about comes from having an awareness and keen understanding of what you know that God has called, created, and ordained you to do. It is about prioritizing purpose, not the relentless pursuit of busyness or what I call a "busy mess!"

Purpose and *calling*—as I am using them—refer to what you believe you were born, gifted, and graced to do. Equally, these are the things in life that potentially create your areas of most significant impact. Purpose and calling are steeped in who we are and how God gets the most glory from our lives. In short, this is how you and I produce so much fruit.

What a privilege and honor it is to be gifted with the ability and passion to give that unique blessing to the world! To neglect, diminish, manipulate, or "pimp" the gift, or allow others to use it deceitfully, is a gross exploitation that reduces us over time, hardens our hearts, and depletes our souls. If we don't realize how important this is, we run the risk of people pleasing or saying yes entirely too much. Furthermore, we live our lives—and our faith—attempting to secure bags that don't belong to us. Even if we have a personality that allows us to bode well under pressure, the effects of this misuse will eventually begin to show. Some consequences may include being and feeling overworked, having decreased productivity while over-performing, loss of passion, constant complaining, and a host of poor choices in our efforts to find relief and release from a self-imposed problem. Ultimately, this behavior leads to destructive habits like neglect of self, health, and relationships.

There are a multitude of reasons many of us are always saying, "Yes." It may be fear of rejection. We could be trying to overcompensate for a perceived failure or reacting to having overbearing relationships during childhood development. Is there a relationship in our adult life that is overbearing? Maybe it is avoidance of a problem that causes us to say "Yes." Instead of creating boundaries, we simply give in to avoid facing something or someone. Is the yes due to the need for approval or attention seeking due to a lack? Even pride, guilt, or our own attempts at manipulation prompt us to say yes far too many times. Think. There could be something on the inside of us that strong-arms into thinking, "I have to... or everything will unravel." Whatever our reasons, it is time to accept that "NO" is good, too, so we can prioritize what is important to God and essential to us.

Prayer:

God, show us why we always say "Yes."
Show us, Holy Spirit. Teach us!
Uproot a thing and kill it. Please give us a
discerning spirit so we can thrive in the
essential "Yes" and say "No" often, too. Amen.

The Scent of a Woman

Luke 7:36-50 KJV

And one of the Pharisees desired him that he would eat with him. And he went into the Pharisee's house, and sat down to meat. And, behold, a woman in the city, which was a sinner, when she knew that Jesus sat at meat in the Pharisee's house, brought an alabaster box of ointment, And stood at his feet behind him weeping, and began to wash his feet with tears, and did wipe them with the hairs of her head, and kissed his feet, and anointed them with the ointment. Now when the Pharisee which had bidden him saw it, he spake within himself, saying, This man, if he were a prophet, would have known who and what manner of woman this is that toucheth him: for she is a sinner.

And Jesus answering said unto him, Simon, I have somewhat to say unto thee. And he saith, Master, say on. There was a certain creditor which had two debtors: the one owed five hundred pence, and the other fifty. And when they had nothing to pay, he frankly forgave them both.

Tell me therefore, which of them will love him most? Simon answered and said, I suppose that he, to whom he forgave most. And he said unto him, Thou hast rightly judged. And he turned to the

> woman, and said unto Simon, Seest thou this
> woman? I entered into thine house, thou gavest me
> no water for my feet: but she hath washed my feet
> with tears, and wiped them with the hairs of her
> head. Thou gavest me no kiss: but this woman
> since the time I came in hath not ceased to kiss my
> feet. My head with oil thou didst not anoint:
> but this woman hath anointed my feet with
> ointment. Wherefore I say unto thee, Her sins,
> which are many, are forgiven; for she loved much:
> but to whom little is forgiven, the same loveth
> little. And he said unto her, Thy sins are forgiven.
> And they that sat at meat with him began to say
> within themselves, Who is this that forgiveth sins
> also? And he said to the woman,
> Thy faith hath saved thee; go in peace.

The beauty industry profits from our misguided, highly marketed, and miscalculated beauty standards. We call that womanhood. We spend so much time looking at images that force us to accept someone else's view of what is beautiful and what a woman looks like. Often, we subject ourselves to all manner of fad diets, shapeshifters, surgical procedures, shots, and implanted body parts to meet those perfect social media culture standards.

Is it the outside that makes me a woman?

What makes a woman a woman? Is it the façade of unbreakable confidence of the stilettos clanking in the halls of corporate America or red-carpet events? Or the independence that comes with making choices that were not available to those who came before us? While choice is nice, and we certainly have come a long way to overcome many -isms, those are not the things that make a woman a woman.

Luke 7:36-50 shows us that Christ looks at the heart. The true fragrance of a woman comes from a heart yielded to Him. The true fragrance of sweet savor of a woman comes from a heart yielded to and forgiven by Christ, our Savior. Jesus is the forgiver of sins.

Luke's gospel reveals the condition of the woman's contrite heart toward the One who forgives much. Literally, the language expresses that she was a woman who was known. Everyone knew of her sin, and, in the text, she was of "questionable" reputation. This woman had a known immoral character. She is the unnamed woman living in oppressive societal standards, identified by her perceived failures.

Have you ever been her?

Have you ever been devoted to the wrong choices and identified by your mess up? Have you ever been labeled by the condition of your heart in moments of weakness? Have you ever been reduced to the sum total of your mistakes, misgivings, or questionable past?

This sister in the Bible was labeled a "hot mess," and everybody knew it! She was unwelcome and unwanted, yet she realized something the others did not. She was a fragrant woman who knew *who* to worship and *how* to worship. She knew to call on the forgiver of sin.

The fragrant woman:
- Has a fixed focus and seeks Christ with her whole heart.
- Understands that a contrite heart before our safe and compassionate God brings forth a sweet-smelling savor in God's nostrils.
- Knows that a fragrance God loves costs something. The fragrant woman in Luke 7 boasted a costly, perfumed oil in a flask. This woman wept, so the oil cost her tears—expressions of joy, pain, or remorse. It cost her the kissing and wiping of Jesus' feet with her tears. This fragrance that God loves cost her humility, status, and notoriety.

Dr. Latisha D. Henry-Reeves

PRAYER:

Thank You, Lord, that Your compassion-filled
healing grace covers us.
Your grace releases us
to worship freely and live fully in You.
Through you, we are restored,
and our lives are a sweet fragrant offering
that permeates the room.

Putty In God's Hands

JEREMIAH 18:1-6 KJV
> *The word which came to Jeremiah from the LORD, saying, Arise, and go down to the potter's house, and there I will cause thee to hear my words. Then I went down to the potter's house, and, behold, he wrought a work on the wheels. And the vessel that he made of clay was marred in the hand of the potter: so he made it again another vessel, as seemed good to the potter to make it. Then the word of the LORD came to me, saying, O house of Israel, cannot I do with you as this potter? saith the LORD. Behold, as the clay is in the potter's hand, so are ye in mine hand, O house of Israel.*

Upon reflection of this familiar passage, I have come to one conclusion: God wants us to be putty in His hands. This is the word given to the prophet *(paraphrased)*: Go and see the visual illustration of what I want you to say to my people. Then, I will talk to you again.[3]

---

[3] Jeremiah 18:1-2

As Jeremiah watched the potter making a clay vessel on the wheel, he saw that the potter had complete liberty to shape, mold, mash, and re-shape, re-mold and re-make the vessel. The potter had the liberty to turn it into the desired vessel of his choice for what he alone knew was its purpose. He knew the manner it would be fit to be used. The vessel was made "as it seemed good to the potter to make.[4]"

Verses 5 and 6 are the verses that arrest me. Even though it was delivered specially for the people of Jewish heritage, I know this is a timeless truth that transcends to everyone who is a part of the Body of Christ. Romans 9:20-21 says so.[5]

In our efforts to always exert our self-sufficiency and independence, make the best, most logical decisions, chart our desired career paths, and declare ourselves captains of our own ships and masters of our fate, we have forsaken a foundational truth of our faith. God wants us to be putty in His hands. Does not the Creator, Ruler, and Sustainer of ALL have the right to have the final say and last word? Does not God direct our paths, influence our behaviors, declare His will over our will, set the standard, order our steps and careers, and demand our time, talents, treasures, congregations, businesses, et cetera?

In today's climate and culture, many have reduced God to the image that is comfortable or palatable. The culture wants God to cater to our wants and categorically supply our needs within our timeframes and allotted personal preferences. And a *woe* goes there! In the grace

---

[4] Jeremiah 18:3-4

[5] Romans 9:20-21 reads, "[20] But who are you, a mere man, to talk back to God? Will what is formed say to the one who formed it, "Why did you make me like this?" [21] Or has the potter no right over the clay, to make from the same lump one piece of pottery for honor and another for dishonor?"

dispensation, that thinking still has grave consequences. The Creator and molder of the clay still gets to decide the shape and purpose of each vessel to make known the riches of His glory and power. Yep! For all who are Bible-believing, we can only conclude that God absolutely wants us to be putty in His hands. That means that we embrace *all* — the totality of whom HE has revealed Himself to be in His word — not just the parts we like.

PRAYER:

> Father, You alone know the way we take.
> You know why and what the end result will be.
> Teach us to be submitted
> to the perfecting work already begun in us.
> Help us trust Your intentions toward us.
> Shape our lives to make more influential
> positive impact for Your kingdom.

We Glory in God!!!
(Foolishness and All)

1 Corinthians 1:26-31 NKJV
For you see your calling, brethren,
that not many mighty, not many noble are called.
But God has chosen the foolish things of the world
to put to shame the wise, and God has chosen the
weak things of the world to put to shame the things
which are mighty. And the base things of the world
and the things which are despised God has chosen,
and the things which are not, to bring to nothing
the things that are. That no flesh should glory in
His presence. But of Him you are in Christ Jesus,
who became for us wisdom from God-- and
righteousness and sanctification and redemption--
that, as it is written,
"He who glories, let him glory in the Lord."

I am so overjoyed to be a part of the Body of Christ because it makes no sense that I made it in. It makes no sense that the Father would still love creation so much after He has been betrayed, disobeyed, rejected, and ignored more often than not. WHAT A LOVE! After all that we have done and all we're going to do, it makes no sense that God would love us enough to send His only begotten Son. God sent Jesus to live and die, to be crucified and afflicted on our behalf so that we might live eternally in God's presence. It is utterly absurd that God would allow us to participate in His divine plan to share His glorious gospel. He has given us the awesome responsibility to share that love, that story, that inexplicable peace and freedom from everywhere to everywhere—even to the ends of the earth! The craziest thing of all is that God didn't choose the lofty—those people who are prioritized by a society that prides itself on living by its own principles and practices according to its own whims. He did not choose those who were able to choose themselves—no matter how much we think so. The truth is that not one of us is capable of choosing ourselves. He chose the foolishness of the world to confound and confuse the wise. Why?

    Why would He do such a thing? Because God alone gets the glory! God alone *deserves* the glory, but because humanity has the tendency to be prideful and arrogant at the slightest glimpse of achievement, God has chosen to flip the script. When God chooses you and I to impact the lives of others in positive ways, He gets the glory. When we live for Him and allow Him to work through us, He gets the glory. When we live in the way that God knows is best and most effective using the gifts and callings He has given, God gets the glory! Sometimes, God is glorified through our jobs and professions as well. At times, those are the chosen vehicles to transport the message. The point is that God uses the most foolish acting things in all of His creation to further the gospel. That's us! We are the ones whom God has given the ability to consciously choose to obey, love, surrender, or vehemently oppose Him. He uses them, us, you, and me, with our flaws, failures, foolishness, and all.

PRAYER:

Thank You, Lord!!!
Amid self-doubt and uncertainties,
You remind us that we are chosen,
and included in the plan. You use us.
You use it all! And we were never chosen
because we could meet the need.
Still, you chose us anyway.

The Power of Peace: On Guard

PHILIPPIANS 4:6-7 NKJV
*Be anxious for nothing but in everything by prayer
and supplication with thanksgiving,
let your request be made known to God,
and the peace of God which surpasses all
understanding will guard your hearts and minds.*

Sometimes, we do not know the power of a thing until we fully experience it. Peace is one of those things. In our society, having peace when encountering hardship or struggle is often viewed as passivity, laziness, or apathy. If we are kingdom citizens who read the word and have been to Bible study more than three times, we should realize that kingdom principles often contradict societal norms. According to Christ, we are not to be consumed by worry and preoccupied with trying to control tomorrow.[6] God does not handle things the same way we do. THANK YOU, GOD!

So, it is with peace.

---

[6] Matthew 6:25-34

In the wake of the turmoil, tragedy, and trial, we just want out! When it comes to sickness, death, financial lack, relationship challenges, and overwhelming disappointment, we just would RATHER NOT. But the truth is that neither the Word of God in written form — the Bible — nor the Living Word — our Christ — ever tells us or gives any indication that life will be completely trouble-free. That is why we are given what we need to endure. We have the Holy Spirit living in us and the word of God working for us. As we become more intimately familiar with God through prayer, reading, and meditating on His word, we become more inclined to trust God and take Him at His word. That is when peace stands guard over our minds.

Apostle Paul wrote about our feet being shod with the gospel of peace from the preparation of the gospel as part of the whole armor of God. Your shield is faith. Truth holds you up, girding you faithfully. The helmet of salvation covers and protects. The righteousness of Christ is boldly displayed across your chest. The sword of the Spirit is wielded against every thought (or situation) that tries to create a stronghold that exalts itself up against the knowledge of God. When trouble lurks, feelings of helplessness and hopelessness surface, and the sword of God's Spirit is there. Spirit slices and dices evil up until these negative emotions, which were once largely looming over the firmament of our thinking and existence, become so small that they are now pebbles under our feet. That comes through prayer and supplication, making our requests known to God, and believing Him to be a Mighty Deliverer, Faithful and True.

That is why I absolutely love the movie *The Book of Eli*. Denzel's character was a portrait of the full armor of God in the craziest of circumstances. He was not an instigator or antagonist, yet Eli was always prepared for whatever came his way. Problems, evil, and people would rise against him. He would not become loud or belligerent in the heat of trouble, but he wielded the sword when necessary—disarming, disemboweling, and destroying the opposition—making them as fools. Now, you may say, "Yes, but something bad happened that he could not change, and it killed him." Still, Eli had an assignment that he knew he must complete. And, until his work was finished, he did not let go; he did not give up; he refused to die. Though critically wounded and the tangible sacred book stolen, the Word of God was so hidden within his heart that he recited it word for word and thought for thought. Then, he lay down, and he died. Nevertheless, that was only after having given his next-generation traveling companion a glimpse at compelling purpose and teaching her how to fight. All this he did while blind and homeless because the power of God's peace was his guard.

Let peace keep guard, traveler. Stay on the journey—purpose calleth.

PRAYER:

> Father, we are grateful that we can lay it all
> at your feet and fully accept the peace
> that passes all understanding.
> It is part of the gift of salvation
> that keeps on giving. May our feet be shod
> and our stance unwavering because
> Your peace guards our hearts and minds.

Call Him

JEREMIAH 33:3 NKJV
Call to Me, and I will answer you,
and show you great and mighty things,
which you do not know.

God speaks through the prophet Jeremiah to charge the people to call out to God because God desires to answer them. There is something about the heart of our God that delights Him to respond to the voice of His children. Call and response is a very familiar practice within the Black Church tradition between preacher and congregation. The preacher "calls" or speaks a point, and the congregants affirm in response. How beautiful it is that God's children call out—whether in praise or pain—and God shows up in response. That is one of the major differences between Christianity and many other religions.

Our God is near us and not afar off or aloof, nor is our God a thought or a series of lofty ideas to be obtained. God is very personal and draws near to those who seek Him—those whose hearts and spirits are broken and contrite. He sees need and steps into that need, that trial, or that trouble in that moment *with* us—even when we caused it ourselves. God steps in and *stays* in even when we fail to see Him in it. Today, God's requirement of us is the same as back then. God wants us to call out to Him, so let us receive what He is offering. Let us trust and follow His way, not our own.

If you want something different to happen in your life amid the trouble you face, call to God. Call out to Him. We would do well to forsake all distractions, issues, habits, failures, and foolishness so we could call to Him. No matter if you cry out with a loud voice or whimper with the faintest heart cry, as long as your call is genuine, God will respond. He will answer. He has spoken it and has therefore obligated Himself to respond to your sincerity.

God says that great and mighty things will be spoken by Him and revealed to us. This translates as things that are inaccessible and unfathomable. When we call out to God, He will tell us things we did not know—secrets and mysteries that change us for all eternity.

I am calling Him today and each day that follows. Who knows what problem He may solve or hurt that He may heal—not just for me, but even for others when I hear God's response to my call.

PRAYER:

> **Speak, Lord,**
> **I am listening;**
> **tell me something good.**

You Will Know

Isaiah 30:21 NKJV
Your ears shall hear a word behind you saying, "This is the way walk in it." Whenever you turn to the right hand or whenever you turn to the left.

In this season, more so than usual, many people seem to be expressing an anxious attitude about the next move of God, the next assignment, which job opportunity or direction to take, etc. I know these things are of major importance to all of us. When we were younger, in our faith walk, we thought life was all about personal, tangible gain. While we need those "things" to survive, we know now that all of *this* is so much bigger than just *that*. There is a deep desire on the inside to avoid making the wrong choice, doing the wrong thing, or doing the right thing with the wrong motives. We now long to live our faith in a way that aligns with God's word and God's heart. That is why this scripture is so encouraging to me, and prayerfully, it also encourages you.

Through the prophet, the people were being encouraged that God would be gracious to them even after their missteps. The prophet shared God's promise that God would teach them the way to go. Through God's guidance, they would know which way to go. Verse nineteen states that God would hear the sound of the cry of the people and answer them.

Beloved, God hears the sounds of our heart's cry to Him, and He answers us by His Spirit and in His time. Jesus said it this way, "When He, the Spirit of truth, has come, He will guide you into all truth; for He will not speak on His own authority, but whatever He hears, He will speak, and He will tell you things to come.[7]"

God has a plan, and since it is His plan and since He created us for Him, then it is God who is responsible for working all things together to get us to the expected end. Our job is to wait, not slothfully in our deeds but with confident anticipation and expectation, all while faithfully doing what we are sure God last instructed us to do. So, rest in His greatness and ability, His faithfulness and sovereignty. God's all-seeing and all-knowingness have not changed. His arm has not grown short! He will not let you veer off course without directing you. He still knows where you are and how to get in touch with you.

Keep praying, and wait on Him, so that when He says, "This is the way," you can walk in it—you can get to stepping.

PRAYER:

**Daddy God, help us believe without doubting,
knowing that You are faithful,
and You always do Your part.
When it is time to move, we will know.
Give us the will to obey.
Amen.**

---

[7] John 16:13

In Everything??

1 THESSALONIANS 5:16-18 NKJV
Rejoice always. Pray without ceasing,
in everything give thanks;
for this is the will of God in Christ Jesus for you.

These days, it seems that evil is much more present, or at least it seems that evil is much more visible. Seemingly, we have more questions than answers. Some find this to be plenty enough reason for them to choose not to believe in God's existence or His power to save, heal, and deliver. Others choose to make a god of their own choosing — an aloof god that looks from afar, not responding to the heart cries of people. They make a god of some*thing* that fits in a cabinet, on a bookshelf, or lives in a tree or prism. Still, others choose to make philosophy their God. They build scientific guesses regarding all matters of humanity, creative culture, and use consciousness to exalt a brazen godlike status — taking and making an idol from a little bit of this and a little bit of that. Of all the reasons that many find (or create) in the world to not believe in God, in these same people — and in their vain attempts to excuse God's power away — I find even more reasons to believe in God's power and existence.

The apostle Paul encourages the church at Thessalonica by laying out the basics of the faith: the message of the gospel and how it applies to the truths that they believe and hold steadfast to. We would do well to read this letter from Paul. In our longing to understand, we ask questions, and when we do not find the answers we seek — or when we disapprove of the answers — we resolve to create something we can accept or readily explain.

I have learned that the word of God provides an answer and a solution for many of life's major ills. Unfortunately, the "fix" just isn't quick enough for us. Having been a person who has gone through tantrums, anxieties, and cryptic, cynical cycles of doubt, fear, unbelief, and outright rebellion, I have realized that the more I submit to the Word and the Spirit of God, the more I mature in faith and understanding. As things happen, I learn to better appreciate the death and resurrection of Christ on behalf of us all. The more I embrace the beauty of the unconditional and inseparable love of the Father for His children, and for the working of the ministry of the Holy Spirit — not just in my life but in the earth — the more thankful I am. And the more grateful I am, the more I share my faith with others.

Naturally, we prefer ease rather than hardship, but it is the hardship of life and its trouble that drives us to pray. Prayer drives us to hear, and hearing drives us to obey. Obedience deepens our faith and relationship with God. As children, when we were overwhelmed or afraid, we would cling to our parents until we knew everything was alright. We trusted our parents, their judgment, and their words. When their words proved true — and even when they didn't — we showered them with hugs and kisses. Then, we praised and protected their names — even to the point of fighting: DON'T talk about my Mama!!! We said, "Please," when there was a need, and we said, "Thank you," when all was taken care of or when we had faith that all would be well.

Whew!

The trusting nature of the child is to stay in communication with the Father by listening and talking, by resting in the truth of His words, and by thanking Him perpetually for everything that He is holding together. We thank Him for everything He is healing, tearing down, rebuilding, and working together for our good. Using this confidence in the Father, don't give up or let go because your circumstance does not look how you expect it to look. Do not give in because you cannot explain why everything happens as it does. Don't create your own god or accept one already created by some lofty thinker because if they can fully understand their god's workings, I promise they are too small, insignificant, and powerless to truly help you with your life. Keep praying and working. Do what you can to contribute to making things better in your corner of the world. After all, it may be bad, but it is NOT as bad as it could be.

Prayer:

**God, in everything, let us give thanks.
Help us to soon find that we have
a lot more to give thanks for.**

He is Still Doing It

1 Thessalonians 5:23-24 NKJV
Now may the God of peace Himself sanctify you
completely, and may your whole spirit, soul,
and body be preserved blameless
at the coming of our Lord Jesus Christ.
He who calls you is faithful, who also will do it.

One of the hardest things for us to do is fully and completely rest in the fact that Jesus Christ has already completed the work.

What work?

Christ's death on the cross incurred the complete wrath of God. God's wrath for sin was poured out on Him on our behalf.[8] Jesus really did die a substitutionary death for the world, for every person. Christ was resurrected, and victory is His and ours. For all who choose to believe in the atoning death and resurrection of Jesus Christ, we do not have to choose a complacent existence because we are so afraid that if we misstep or mess up, we are

---

[8] Romans 5:8-9

doomed. Let's face this fact head-on: Believers will mess up, make the wrong choice, and miss the mark. However, when we mess up, there is grace because of Christ's death and resurrection. Still, this is not at all an excuse to live haphazardly. We must confess our shortcomings, turn from the wrong direction to the right path, and keep moving forward without condemning ourselves.[9]

We, who believe, have also received the Spirit of Christ—the Holy Spirit who has sealed us and is our guarantee.[10] With those things in mind, let us not grow weary and be yoked by legalism and self-condemnation nor by the condemnation from another. Let us walk in the liberty of Christ while living the sanctified life.

To be sanctified means we are selected by God for uncommon use, for a sacred purpose, and for service to advance the Kingdom of God. Our purpose, use, and service are to seek to live according to the call, yet it is God who sanctifies us completely. JEHOVAH MEKADDISHKEM (the Lord who Sanctifies)![11]

God knows our strengths AND our weaknesses. Through the beauty of God's grace, Jesus' work, the Word's washing, and the Holy Spirit's keeping, we will be preserved, blameless: body, spirit, and soul. He who called you is faithful. Every promise God has spoken, God is able to keep, and HE WILL DO IT!

PRAYER:

> **God, we rejoice that You are faithful,
> and there is no shadow of turning
> nor any deception in You.
> We take You at your word.**

---

[9] Romans 8:1
[10] Ephesians 1:13-14
[11] 1 John 1:7; Psalm 119:1

Give Them What You've Got

ACTS 3:6-7 NKJV
*Then Peter said, "Silver and gold I do not have,
but what I do have I give you:
In the name of Jesus Christ of Nazareth,
rise up and walk.
And he took him by the right hand
and lifted him up and immediately
his feet and ankle bones received strength.*

We should not miss the opportunity to be a blessing. We must fasten our eyes on the need in our community and opportunities to help. Stop, look, listen, and discern. Slow down a little and take a look around. All of us can do something for someone — something that will make a difference. Don't miss the chance to help by being too busy and too preoccupied. Within us, God does more than we can imagine; With our little, God makes much.[12]

Let us not be afraid to look opportunity in the eye. It isn't rocket science; it's opportunity. Somehow, we have

---

[12] See Ephesians 3:20.

become intimidated by the challenges our communities face and stopped recognizing them as opportunities to have a positive impact on the lives of others. We can't freely live our lives if we lead in fear. The Holy Spirit knows what we have to offer. With these gifts, we must choose to help others with the challenges at hand.

I believe that is why certain people cross our paths at different times in our lives. Life offers a series of exchanges whereby we have a chance to give, share with others, and speak and sow kindness into their lives. Mentoring a young person, sharing a kind word of encouragement, and giving a drink of water or a plate of food are all small kindnesses in our eyes, but they are of major long-term impact on someone else. Sometimes, we must look past the exterior, hard places, and anything that makes us uncomfortable in order to meet the needs of others. This is not about money. As a matter of fact, in the biblical text, Paul says they didn't have any.

As for us, we have unparalleled benefits: resurrection power, peace that passes understanding, the ability to endure and overcome, and faith that moves mountains. Give these to others in practical ways based on your resources, and don't focus so much on what you *don't* have.

Give 'em whatcha got!
God does the rest.

PRAYER:

**Father, help us give away freely,
just as You have given to us.
Take our little and make much of it
so that Your Name is exalted.
Amen.**

What Does Jesus Do?

Remember "WWJD?" This mantra stood for "What Would Jesus Do?" It served as a reminder to each person who wore the bracelet, t-shirt, or carried the key chain (and to all who saw the logo) to stop and consider Christ when making decisions and doing life daily. When preparing for this study entry, I thought in a similar manner. However, my question is, "What *Does* Jesus Do?"

HEBREWS 10:21-23 NKJV
*and having a High Priest over the house of God,
let us draw near with a true heart in full assurance
of faith, having our hearts sprinkled from an evil
conscience and our bodies washed with pure water.
Let us hold fast the confession of our hope
without wavering, for He who promised is faithful.
And let us consider one another in order to
stir up love and good works, not forsaking
the assembling of ourselves together,
as is the manner of some, but exhorting
one another, and so much the more
as you see the Day approaching*

I believe the writer of Hebrews was helping to convey the fact that there is assurance of your confession. Jesus Christ's work is the very foundation of our faith. Jesus is the High Priest who offered the sacrifice. Jesus is the savior who *is* the sacrifice! Hebrews 4:14-16 tells us that He passed through the heavens and appeared in God's presence on our behalf! He knows our weaknesses and sympathizes with us. Because of what He has done, we can come boldly to the throne of grace.

What Jesus did then—and what He continually does for all of us—is the picture of what love is! That alone is fuel for the fire of your faith! Hebrews informs us that Christ's sacrifice surpasses the blood of bulls and goats. Animals were sacrificed on behalf of the people's sins, but since people sin perpetually, these sacrifices could never be enough. Even with these sacrifices, weighty reminders of their sins remained with the people.

Our joy in Jesus is this: as our High Priest who came to offer sacrifice for us, Jesus became the sacrifice for us to put sin away once and for all. Jesus' sacrifice destroyed the hold, the weight, and power of sin.[13] Jesus did that then, and His saving power is still doing it now. It was appointed for Christ to die, and His shed blood still works—it will never lose its power! Jesus sacrificed His life so that we could live.

Christ keeps us in right standing before the Father. He keeps us in the beauty of God's presence without fear of wrath, condemnation, guilt, or stain. Christ prays and pleads our case.[14] The Greek word used in these verses means to plead, intercede, and make an appeal for

---

[13] See Hebrews 9:26; Hebrews 7:27; 9:12, 24-28; 10:1-2, 10, 12, 14; 13:12.

[14] The following texts tell how Jesus intercedes on our behalf: Hebrews 6:19-20; 10:19-22; Luke 23:45; Hebrews 7:25; Romans 8:34.

someone. Jesus Christ did that then, and He is still doing it for us right now. He did it then, when we were enemies of God, and He's still interceding while we are yet sinners.[15] Don't miss this! Jesus is *still* stepping in on our behalf, nullifying the accusations and plans of the evil one, the accuser, Satan, the father of lies.

This is a reminder to think on what Jesus did and what Jesus does. Now, run on a little further in life, bless someone else, and hold on a lil' while longer.

THIS IS GOOD NEWS!!!

PRAYER:

> **Daddy God, help us to meditate on
> what Jesus did and does
> so we gladly tell somebody else.**

---

[15] Romans 5:8-11

I Wanna Be Yours

Jeremiah 24:7 NKJV
Then I will give them a heart to know Me,
that I am the Lord; and they shall be My people,
and I will be their God,
for they shall return to Me with their whole heart.

I am aware that God was speaking to His chosen people concerning judgment for their disobedience, but I am stopped in my tracks by the beauty of God's love for His children—even after they've messed up. Jeremiah was not just bringing corrective declaration and rebuke, but he came bearing a tender word of restoration and reconciliation. Jeremiah spoke of hope for a people—and future generations—who desperately needed it.

Now, this restoration wouldn't happen immediately. The consequences of the people's actions would not just disappear, but their restoration was guaranteed because God is trustworthy. The people would certainly be restored in the fullness of time. This is good news for me and for us, and it makes me glad.

The consequences of my bad choices were evident in failed, toxic relationships or unnecessary debt, but the hope of restoration was certain. My life's restoration was guaranteed because God always watches over His promises to make sure they are fulfilled. God's promises for His sons and daughters shall come to pass. That is why we put everlasting hope in God.

We are often still apt to hold God hostage to our expectations and desires. Then, when He does not comply, we abandon—even if momentarily—God and God's cause in exchange for what seems more profitable, popular, or easier to deal with and manage. We abandon God for something that yields what we feel to be a valuable return or more practicality. BIG MISTAKE!!! Or—more blatantly put—this is sinful and frequently detrimental to us! When we are displeased and disgruntled about God not fulfilling our expectations or wrongfully perceiving something else is better, we tend to stray from God in our hearts.

Isn't it wonderful to know that our God—who is strong, mighty, awesome in power, and perfect in all His ways—is always seeking restoration? He reconciled His people unto Himself, so even when you haven't dotted every i or crossed every t, He is still there waiting with a word of restoration. When you've had a temporary lapse of judgment, or you have found that your heart has strayed away from the things of God, He is still there, waiting. For the remnant, it was God's will for them to return to Him so the new covenant could be written on their hearts. The new covenant was to tell them that God wants them whole-heartedly no matter what. God's very best—Jesus Christ—is the fulfillment of that prophecy. My, my, my! What a love! God loves with an everlasting love. Because of that fulfillment of the promise, you and I have Christ Jesus as Savior and King.

Just like the remnant, you and I must know that God's love is greater than any issue or failure we have committed. God stands to offer freely to us all the fullness of a healed and restored heart that He will indeed be our God, and we will be His people.

PRAYER:

O most Holy, Holy God,
What a beautiful love this is.
With all that I am or am not,
all that I've done or have not,
Lord, I wanna be yours.
I am yours and
I am in awestruck wonder that You are mine.

What's the Goal?

JAMES 1:2-8 NKJV

*My brethren, count it all joy when you fall into various trials, knowing that the testing of your faith produces patience. But let patience have its perfect work, that you may be perfect and complete, lacking nothing. If any of you lacks wisdom, let him ask of God, who gives to all liberally and without reproach, and it will be given to him. But let him ask in faith, with no doubting, for he who doubts is like a wave of the sea driven and tossed by the wind.
For let not that man suppose that he will receive anything from the Lord; he is a double-minded man, unstable in all his ways.*

I so appreciate a conversation I had the other day with a dear friend of mine. Anyone who intimately knows me knows that I do not profess to have "already attained it," but I indeed press toward the mark of the prize of the high calling. I want to press until the day of pressing is over, but I—like most people I know—would not be the first to stand in line to suffer voluntarily.

Suffering, hardship, trials, and tragedy are not on anyone's list of favorite things to do, but the more I experience — and the more I learn from the Word of God — I see that these things are just a part of life. Theoretically, we do not seem to have a problem with this reality until the suffering hits our street, family, or household. During these times of travail, the questions and accusations against the character and nature of our holy, sovereign Creator speak louder than Sunday morning and Wednesday (or whatever day your congregation holds Bible study or mid-week service ☺).

This is not a judgment but an observation by a fellow traveler who has asked many questions and voiced many complaints to God and some trusted friends. Whether they are of our making or just "happenstance," suffering and trials of any kind can be traumatizing and debilitating, so it is not my intent to make light of them nor to try to explain every uncomfortable plight of the human experience. I cannot do that and will not endeavor to; I am not God. What I can offer is the wisdom that — for committed followers of Christ — there is a goal that hardship seeks to achieve.

The goal of the most dreaded and painful moments — suffering, lessons, experiences — is that we will GROW UP, simply put. It sounds a little harsh when I say it to myself, but I cannot deny its truth. When the text says to be perfect and lacking nothing, this does not suggest perfection in the way we think of perfection. The text does not suggest that — after a particular instance of suffering is over — God is going to "reward" you with the restoration of every single thing you have ever lost. This excerpt is not saying that all riches and financial wealth will be restored or brought to you, nor does it propose that neither you nor anyone you know will be immune to cancer, other sickness, or mortal disaster. God does, however, make exceeding great promises in the Word to

God's people. Still, God alone decides and disperses different types of blessings according to His work and will in us.

What the text actually explains is the purpose of trials in a believer who is whole and complete, mature in faith, and confident in God's ability and faithfulness. James suggests that enduring hardship and allowing patience to have its work in us will bring eternal reward and make us one of the "first fruits" of God's creatures.

SO...

What does that mean?

It means we must be the type of believers who persevere through trouble, trials, suffering, and hardship with confidence in the character and nature of our great and faithful God! We must have faith in the authority and work of Christ and in the keeping, transformative, and dynamite power of the Holy Spirit. We must do this even if we have to cry, even if we have questions, and even if we do not understand or agree. All in all, to be fully pleasing, we must remember that we are consecrated to God by God for God.

The goal is that we grow up and mature in God whether we receive the desired tangible outcome or not.

Prayer:

**Lord, may we embrace the reality that our lives
are an offering of worship
and an example to this world,
for You to use as You wish.
Mature us,
and shine the light of Your glory.**

What If God Doesn't and You Don't

DANIEL 3:16-18 NKJV
> Shadrach, Meshach, and Abed-Nego answered
> and said to the king, "O Nebuchadnezzar,
> we have no need to answer you in this matter.
> If that is the case, our God whom we serve
> is able to deliver us from the burning fiery furnace,
> and He will deliver us from your hand, O king.
> But if not, let it be known to you, O king,
> that we do not serve your gods, nor will we
> worship the gold image which you have set up."

We spend so much time encouraging one another in one direction that, many times, we do not stop to consider, "What if that is not the direction God decides to take?" Or, "What if I do not get what I want most?" Who discusses this? Now let me put this disclaimer here because I do realize that:

GOD CAN, GOD WILL, and GOD DOES!!!
GOD'S DELAY IS NOT GOD'S DENIAL!
GOD IS FAITHFUL TO FULFILL EVERY PROMISE!
GOD'S PROMISES ARE YEA AND AMEN...

What I want us to think through are the times when our desires, goals, wishes, and hopes are not evil nor sinful. *Still*, sometimes they are *not* God's plan, nor His design, for our lives individually. What if God does not co-sign our vision, our dream, or our request? Here are some examples.

- With sincere motive, David desired to build a house for God to dwell in. It was a good idea—even the prophet thought so, but God said "No." [16] God's plan for David and his future was far greater and more important for all eternity. God made David a house. The Lion of the tribe of Judah, the Messiah, the Christ, is the forever dynasty of David's house. David *is* a house. That is better than building one—no matter how big and beautiful the temple was. NO ONE else has that testimony or covenant promise made directly to them by God, but many are the beneficiaries of the direction God decided to take in David's life.

- Acts 16:6-10 finds the Apostle Paul forbidden by the Holy Spirit to preach the word in one place. Instead, Paul is redirected by the Spirit to go to Macedonia. Certainly, it was a good idea to preach the gospel. After all, Paul was called to preach the gospel to the Gentiles. However, at that time, God wanted Paul elsewhere, preaching the gospel. The reward of Paul's obedience is ginormous, to say the least.

I know we may not want to admit it, but maybe you and I are so uncomfortable because God wants to do something *greater* through us. Perhaps God wants to create a greater legacy and have a more powerful and widespread impact than what we imagine possible.

---

[16] See 2 Samuel 7.

I am writing while enduring the tension of these things in my own life. Lest you believe I am talking *at* you, I am not! I am talking to *myself*. I am walking *with* you on this path that "feels" like a journey to ambiguity. Notice that I placed the word *feels* in quotes because feelings are very fickle. During challenging times, feelings are subject to change in a moment. They are subject to meaning which is under the influence of something else. Feelings are under the control of whatever influences us at a particular time.

Sooo...

How about we stop hanging our hopes on—and being subject to—things that may change at any given moment? Let us decide to stand in the truth and power of our God, who is absolutely unchangeable, does not fail, and cannot lie. Let us trust in He who is, and was, and is to come—He who is forever and forever will be. This is our God, whose love is unconditional, whose gaze is fixed on us, and who is concerned about every single thing that concerns us. Let us refine our trust in Our God, who simply speaks, and all that was *not* moves to what *is*, and after all that, time still stands! This is our God whose IS-NESS makes *us* His business—our one, true God whose being, in three persons, high jacks our understanding, yet He necessitates and validates our purpose for life on this planet. This is the God who lets us participate in something BIGGER than we can fathom, so why would we *not* trust God?

If I believe that God is, and that God does all of the above, shouldn't I know that what is conceived in God's mind is better than what is conceived in mine?

PRAYER:

Lord, I am thankful that You alone know the way that we take. We will choose to trust You no matter the outcomes or the unmet expectations of our wants.

Yes, God Can Use You

Acts is the New Testament book that provides a bold display of the working of the Holy Spirit. Paul (formerly known as Saul) is the perfect example of this work.

ACTS 9:17-19, 29-31 NKJV

And Ananias went his way and entered the house; and laying his hands on him he said, "Brother Saul, the Lord Jesus, who appeared to you on the road as you came, has sent me that you may receive your sight and be filled with the Holy Spirit." Immediately there fell from his eyes something like scales, and he received his sight at once; and he arose and was baptized.

So when he had received food, he was strengthened. Then Saul spent some days with the disciples at Damascus.

And he spoke boldly in the name of the Lord Jesus and disputed against the Hellenists, but they attempted to kill him. When the brethren found out, they brought him down to Caesarea and sent him out to Tarsus.

Dr. Latisha D. Henry-Reeves

The Church Prospers

> *Then the churches throughout all Judea, Galilee, and Samaria had peace and were edified. And walking in the fear of the Lord and in the comfort of the Holy Spirit, they were multiplied.*

Read that again. Take note of what God was able to do with a man who used to be one of the chief offenders against what Christ had come to do. When we allow God's revelation to work *on* us, we then allow God to work *through* us. We learn several things from scriptures like these, which partially display Paul's life:

- The past does not dictate our future, nor does the past condemn us to the past. Reread that. Read it again.
- What you learned in a past season gives you an advantage in other seasons, if you let it.
- Pain is part of the plan. However, pain is not a perpetual punishment that you deserve to endure for the rest of your life due to your past. Look at pain as a motivator indicating that change needs to happen or that change is happening in the moment you are feeling pain.
- When we move with God, God will produce God's exceedingly abundant results.

PRAYER:

Daddy God, we yield even when we don't know the *how*, the *when*, or the *way*, but we do know that great things are always in Your will.

Increase Anyway

Exodus 1:12 NKJV
But the more they afflicted them,
the more they multiplied and grew.
And they were in dread of the children of Israel.

The Bible says that after Joseph died, there arose a king who cared nothing about Joseph's legacy as an honorable, wise leader of integrity nor his people. The wicked Pharoah cared to know nothing about the God of Joseph nor the favor that was once resting on Joseph's kindred. Instead, he oppressed those of Joseph's lineage — the Hebrews, who were eventually called Israelites. God's people — who were chosen to be a light and point other nations to God — were forced to serve as Egyptian slaves.

This passage shows us some of the things that still ring true:

- Everyone will not celebrate you.
  All of the people who you journey with will not be happy for your successes or your perseverance. Increase anyway!

- Π Increase is a choice.
  Choose today. The children of Israel multiplied and were exceedingly fruitful. They produced and reproduced with what they had despite the harsh inhumane circumstances.
- Π Go with God and grow.
  Because they were chosen by God Himself, the Israelites had a deposit of something within them that made them keep going even when they could have given up. How much more is this true with the Holy Spirit living within us? Holy Spirit reminds us that greater is He who resides within believers than the evil that lives within the systems and powers of this wicked world.

For you, the encouragement is resolve to THRIVE! Get Up! *Live!* Produce and reproduce because God's purpose always prevails! Partner with God by aligning your faith with God's promises. Where there is doubt, ask for help with your unbelief. Google scriptures that encourage you in the areas of your doubt. Write out a list of affirmations derived from what God says about the matter. Start right where you are. Use what you have and build from there and watch God increase in you and expand your territory. Perseverance pays off. God has a way of turning things around by turning around even the ugly things for our good and for God's glory.

PRAYER:

**God, You are strong and mighty
even when we face the toughest situations.
Teach us to remember that we can LIVE because
Christ lives in us. We belong to You, God.
We are chosen in Christ Jesus before the world
began. We are signed, sealed and delivered—
fortified with power. We have no need to
diminish ourselves, shrink back, or disappear.**

Qualified by God

NUMBERS 27:5-8 NKJV
So Moses brought their case before the Lord.
And the Lord spoke to Moses, saying:
"The daughters of Zelophehad speak what is right;
you shall surely give them a possession of
inheritance among their father's brothers, and
cause the inheritance of their father to pass to them.
And you shall speak to the children of Israel,
saying: 'If a man dies and has no son, then you
shall cause his inheritance to pass to his daughter.

Every time I read this passage, I smile. I thank God and meditate on His goodness to me — to us. This story is a testament to God's authority and ability to do whatever God wants. It paints a portrait that shows us that God dispenses favor, however, God wants, to whomever God chooses. Culturally, this result was not the expected outcome. Zelophehad had no sons, so his daughters stood before Moses and asked for property because their father died in the wilderness. Traditionally, this property — which would have been given to his relatives — would not have been divided among the females of his clans. It would have been divided among the sons first, and then distributed to other male relatives. Culturally, it was deemed unfortunate to die and have no sons, but guess what? God is not bound by cultural norms! Aren't we glad? There are many instances where we see God foregoing cultural norms and traditions. God is He who makes the last first and the first last. He provides for the least, the lost, and the disenfranchised. God lifts the poor, frees the oppressed, proclaims the year of jubilee, and He demolishes classism, sexism, and nationalism. I get super excited just thinking about it! God can shift it all in a second!

That's what we see happening here with Zelophehad's daughters. Although having female beneficiaries of inheritance was not customary in the culture of this day, God turned it around and said *change it*. What we see is God bringing about equity and leveling the playing field. God does that through people. Through the lives of these formidable women, we see God disturbing systems. Zelophehad's daughters were resolute enough to stay on the journey—a journey that was not easy—and they were bold enough to ask for what should be rightfully theirs. Their story teaches that we have a choice in how we respond to what happens around us. We learn three things from Zelophehad's daughters:

- Π *Decide!*
  Even when the odds are against you, use the example of Zelophehad's daughters, who *decided* to thrive in an unfortunate situation.
- Π *Ask for what you need!*
  It was the boldness to *ask* that got a favorable response.
- Π *Do not disqualify yourself* from the blessing!
  Bet on God, who qualifies, validates, and vindicates. God used Zelophehad's daughters— the unqualified female heirs to secure the

promise — to pioneer change and set a precedent as the new standard.

PRAYER:

Thank You for being Our God who qualifies, quantifies, and clarifies to bring about necessary change for Your glory and our advancement.

Joy Will Come

RUTH 1:20-21; 4:13-16 NKJV

> *But she said to them, "Do not call me Naomi; call me Mara, for the Almighty has dealt very bitterly with me. I went out full, and the Lord has brought me home again empty. Why do you call me Naomi, since the Lord has testified against me, and the Almighty has afflicted me?"*
>
> *So Boaz took Ruth and she became his wife; and when he went in to her, the Lord gave her conception, and she bore a son. Then the women said to Naomi, "Blessed be the Lord, who has not left you this day without a close relative; and may his name be famous in Israel! And may he be to you a restorer of life and a nourisher of your old age; for your daughter-in-law, who loves you, who is better to you than seven sons, has borne him." Then Naomi took the child and laid him on her bosom, and became a nurse to him. Also the neighbor women gave him a name, saying, "There is a son born to Naomi." And they called his name Obed. He is the father of Jesse, the father of David.*

Dr. Latisha D. Henry-Reeves

I remember hearing my grandmother and my mother saying, "God moves in mysterious ways." I was a child and did not know what that declaration meant back then. Now, I do. In the book of Ruth, we see the mysterious hand of God moving only after a series of personal tragedies in the lives of Naomi, Ruth, and Orpah. Ruth and Orpah, Naomi's daughters-in-law, lost their husbands. Naomi lost her husband and her sons. I can't imagine the insurmountable grief she experienced, and to make matters even worse, they lived in a time and culture where men were the primary financial providers. Naomi felt hopeless and helpless. Orpah returned to her people. Ruth and Naomi went to Bethlehem.

This study of tragedy-to-triumph shows us that God brings restoration when we choose joy. Although it is not easy, when we release the power of the pain and seek another perspective, joy awaits.

In your life, focus on what matters. Do not only focus on what hurts right now. Look at what you have instead of burying your hopes alongside what you lost. Choose joy even when you don't get all you want.

Naomi ultimately decided to choose joy when she mentored and prepared her daughter-in-law to be redeemed by Boaz. While Naomi never got her husband nor her sons back, she chose to see hope in the joy of a kinsman redeemer. We should do so as well; our Kinsman Redeemer has secured the joy of our future for all eternity. We choose joy!

Prayer:

**Lord, we are thankful that we can choose joy.
You alone can work all things together to bring
a new perception and revelation of life
and goodness that comes out
of even the harshest storms.
Teach us to anticipate and embrace joy,
one moment, one encounter, one day at a time.**

Life Lessons from a Dark Place

DANIEL 2:46-49 NKJV

Daniel and His Friends Promoted in a Strange Land

Then King Nebuchadnezzar fell on his face, prostrate before Daniel, and commanded that they should present an offering and incense to him. The king answered Daniel, and said, "Truly your God is the God of gods, the Lord of kings, and a revealer of secrets, since you could reveal this secret." Then the king promoted Daniel and gave him many great gifts; and he made him ruler over the whole province of Babylon, and chief administrator over all the wise men of Babylon. Also Daniel petitioned the king, and he set Shadrach, Meshach, and Abed-Nego over the affairs of the province of Babylon; but Daniel sat in the gate of the king.

Judah was conquered by Babylon, with King Nebuchadnezzar taking the best and brightest to conform them and assimilate them into the Babylonian culture and serve his kingdom. Daniel, Shadrach, Meshach, and Abed-nego were chosen to serve the king in a culture where their God wasn't served, worshipped, or recognized. It was a dark place. Not only was their God not worshipped, but they were torn from the land to which their promise was attached. I am sure there was great sorrow and confusion attached to their circumstance. For them, this had to be a dark place.

Here are some points to ponder:
- Daniel's life and faithful service spoke for him.
- Daniel had a resolve to follow God even in a dark place.
- Daniel served with integrity of heart.
- Daniel was consistent with God and man.
- Daniel did not become bitter but continued in prayer and consecrated service in darkness. Because of Daniel's faithfulness, he was prepared to step up when an opportunity arose. He could hear from God and was available to be used by God, so Daniel interpreted the king's dream with such conviction and certainty that the enemy knew Daniel's God was the God of gods and Lord of kings.

Here are some key takeaways:
- Daniel resolved and persevered in prayer, in an intimate relationship with God. In the integrity of heart, his life spoke.
- Daniel did not defile himself in order to promote himself. He was found faithfully serving. His goal wasn't selfish advancement; it was faithfulness to God.
- Daniel did not forget Shadrach, Meshach or Abed-nego when promotion came. He'd journeyed with them, suffered with them in exile, learned of this new culture with them, and he also remembered their faithfulness

on the journey. He spoke up about their value and character. Four of them were to be promoted because of one of them. We must not let position and promotion cause us to forget or forsake other journey dwellers. There's room for *all* of us to advance, not just *one* of us. God brings promotion to advance all, not just one, for a greater impact and for His glory. Daniel remembers this even as he becomes administrator over all the king's wise men and overseer of kingdom affairs!

π Although they did nothing to warrant being in exile, Daniel DID NOT become bitter, and neither did his fellow journey dwellers. Through it all, they were faithful. They remained faithful, loyal, and diligent in their service while in circumstances they had no control over and despite the trouble they didn't deserve.

π Daniel never lost sight of who he was or to whom he belonged; He belonged to God. Daniel knew that God was responsible for him, his life, his people, and his promotion, even in a dark place with a wicked king. Which leads to this:

You DON'T NEED TO vilify them
in order to validate you!!!
When God brings promotion and fulfills
promises for your destiny,
let your life speak!
God speaks through our lives
to bring glory to God.
It's all about God and not us.

God sees us in dark places and The Light shines brightest in darkness especially when we reflect God's glory and God's will as we move forward. God is always working, even in the darkness, so we know God holds the heart of the king in His hand and can turn it around whenever—and wherever—He wishes. Keep this in mind, and remember, we can all be *big*, together. We are born, increased in, and made for community. There will always be fellow journey dwellers, even in a dark place.

PRAYER:

> **Father, remind us that**
> **You shine brightest**
> **in the darkness.**
> **No matter how dark it gets,**
> **You are working through us**
> **in every place we are.**

God of the Victory

1 Samuel 17: 45-47 NKJV
> Then David said to the Philistine, "You come to me with a sword, with a spear, and with a javelin. But I come to you in the name of the Lord of hosts, the God of the armies of Israel, whom you have defied. This day the Lord will deliver you into my hand, and I will strike you and take your head from you. And this day I will give the carcasses of the camp of the Philistines to the birds of the air and the wild beasts of the earth, that all the earth may know that there is a God in Israel. Then all this assembly shall know that the Lord does not save with sword and spear; for the battle is the Lord's, and He will give you into our hands."

ITS ALWAYS A CHOICE!!

Scary is a part of advancement!

The very sight of Goliath was intimidating. His armor was scary. Both Goliath's name and the place Goliath lived are derived from the word that means, "what intimidates." This giant is true to his origin and his naming. Goliath is a crushing, pressing, bully who exposes and uncovers the nakedness of others by creating captive situations which exploit their vulnerability. And after the giant does all of that, his goal is to take his foes captive, into exile and far from freedom. Of course, this was frightening, but not to the young shepherd David, whose eyes were fixed on the power of God and His covenant relationship, not the size of the giant. The lessons of David within this fight apply readily to our lives. Here are the notes:

- FLIP THE SCRIPT!
  Rethink and reframe the situation in your mind. The narrative you tell yourself must be shifted. Intentionally pursue a different perspective. Instead of letting fear become paralyzing, you must let fear become fuel for change.
- RECALL OUR VICTORIES!
  This *ain't* your first rodeo. Remind yourself of times when God has delivered and strengthened you before. Trust God to do it again.
- LIVE STRATEGICALLY!
  We all know that trouble doesn't last always, but trouble is always going to come. Live life with a strategy to handle and overcome each struggle as it comes. Increase your strategic prayer and topical Bible study moments. Employ affirmations based on your favorite scriptures and do some journaling. Your thoughts are a wonderful starting place for strategic reflection.
- USE YOUR POWER!
  Because God is with you in your fight, five smooth stones and a slingshot have untold power. To the other warriors watching the battle, those five stones looked like nothing. What we learn from David is that God can bring certain victory using what looks like "nothing" to us.
- KNOW THAT GOD IS ABLE!

Ephesians 3:20 says God is able to do exceedingly abundantly above all we could ask or think because of the power of Christ at work in us.

PRAYER:

> **All powerful and all-knowing God,
> who has given us the victory,
> we glory in You because,
> no matter what arises,
> victory is certain in You.**

Rest in His Love

Romans 8:37-39 NKJV
Yet in all these things we are more than conquerors
through Him who loved us.
For I am persuaded that neither death nor life,
nor angels nor principalities nor powers,
nor things present nor things to come,
nor height nor depth, nor any other created thing,
shall be able to separate us from the love of God
which is in Christ Jesus our Lord.

I have looked for love in all the wrong places and in many of the wrong people during different seasons in my life as a younger woman. Over time, I found that I changed. I rethought my poor choices and ran like the wind away from the wrong people and the problems. Sometimes. Other times, people changed. Now, here I am, overwhelmed by tears of joy, knowing that Jesus will never change.

How does the unconditional, unwavering love of God inspire you? Personally, I am comforted by knowing that God's love is constant, consistent, and wholly reliable. God is dependable, and He is completely faithful. There is no shadow of turning in Him. That frees us to walk with Him and live for Him. It gives us peace to walk confidently because HE IS even when we are not. God's love is true. He is unfailing, even when we trip, stumble, or fall. Jesus saves, redeems, heals, delivers, strengthens, sets free, and restores because of love, not because of performance, not because of excellence, not because of experience, and not because of pedigree, class, title, or history. He saves us simply because of love—no more performance. Now, you can rest in His love.

PRAYER:

God, we worship You.
We love You because You first loved us.
May we rest in the safety of Your love.

Chart the Course

JUDGES 4:4–8 NKJV

Now Deborah, a prophetess, the wife of Lapidoth, was judging Israel at that time. And she would sit under the palm tree of Deborah between Ramah and Bethel in the mountains of Ephraim. And the children of Israel came up to her for judgment. Then she sent and called for Barak the son of Abinoam from Kedesh in Naphtali, and said to him, "Has not the Lord God of Israel commanded, 'Go and deploy troops at Mount Tabor; take with you ten thousand men of the sons of Naphtali and of the sons of Zebulun; and against you I will deploy Sisera, the commander of Jabin's army, with his chariots and his multitude at the River Kishon; and I will deliver him into your hand'?"

And Barak said to her, "If you will go with me, then I will go; but if you will not go with me, I will not go!"

Can we be honest here?

Deborah was a bad somebody. She was humble enough to seek God's face and bold enough to speak

God's wisdom in a time when there was no king and everyone did what was right in their own eyes. We find Deborah's story in the book of Judges. She was both a prophetess and a judge. It was not customary for women to be judges, but isn't it just like God to use one least expected for God's glory? In this generation, that pioneer could be you. You may have to pioneer the movement, found the organization, take the lead, write the book, start the business, or start the church. Whatever the call, walk it out. Chart the course and lead the way.

Barak said to Deborah, "I won't go unless you go with me." Know that somebody is awaiting your arrival and shift the narrative. It hasn't been done before simply because it wasn't done before. Nothing was done until someone first did it. That someone might be you, so go the distance. Wherever God says go, God leads, and victory is certain no matter what it looks like.

PRAYER:

We know You specialize in doing new things, God. Whatever You want to do in this season, we choose to partner with You.
Speak Lord.
Here we are.
We will go.

Gratefulness

Luke 17:11-19 NKJV

Now it happened as He went to Jerusalem that He passed through the midst of Samaria and Galilee. Then as He entered a certain village, there met Him ten men who were lepers, who stood afar off. And they lifted up their voices and said, "Jesus, Master, have mercy on us!" So when He saw them, He said to them, "Go, show yourselves to the priests." And so it was that as they went, they were cleansed.

And one of them, when he saw that he was healed, returned, and with a loud voice glorified God, and fell down on his face at His feet, giving Him thanks. And he was a Samaritan.

This text shows us that God's goodness is experienced because God is good, not because we are. Ten lepers were cleansed, but only one grateful *former* leper came back.

It is easy to look at the actions of others and judge them harshly, but how often do we do the same? Here's the time for some honest reflection: How often are we recipients of blessings great and small, recipients of new mercies daily, recipients of God's provision of daily bread, and come-through-in-the-eleventh-hour types of blessings? Still, we often neglect to say thank you, right?

There are times when one can simply take God's goodness for granted, even if unintentionally. This is a reminder that we should always be intentional about giving God thanks. Church mothers, grandmothers, and aunties above sixty ought to stand up and say, "You had better say thank you; it's just good manners." It is a best practice to tell the Lord, "Thank you," because God *has done*, *is doing*, and *will do* so much that we benefit from. Gratefulness should be our posture. Think on these things as you read the scripture excerpt again:

- We must praise intentionally.
- Jesus did not require an audit of their past to heal them. God is good because God is good, even when circumstances are not.
- As they were going on their way, the lepers were healed. Our healing often requires obedient participation for the manifestation.
- An obedient, grateful heart comes back to the feet of Jesus, overwhelmed by wonderful change. Christ healed, restored, and canceled the assignment of an evil that robbed its victims of community and stole their joy and their productive futures. A grateful heart remembers to give thanks for the present and the promise of new possibilities.

Prayer:

**Lord Jesus, may our hearts overflow
with grateful praise and adoration
because You did it,
but You didn't have to.**

It Shall Come Forth

ISAIAH 66:9 NKJV
> "Shall I bring to the time of birth,
> and not cause delivery?" says the Lord.
> "Shall I who cause delivery shut up the womb?"
> says your God.

God shall bring forth. It shall come quickly. After the time of preparation, after the time of stretching, after the time of nurture and development, it is God who shall bring forth, in an unusual move and manner. God WILL produce the guaranteed return on the investment God has deposited in you. AFTER the gestation.

Before she was in labor, she gave birth; before her pain, she delivered a male child. Who has heard such a thing? Who has seen such things? Shall the earth be made to give birth in one day? Or shall a nation be born at once? For as soon as Zion was in labor, she gave birth to her children.

> "Shall I bring to the time of birth,
> and not cause delivery?" says the Lord.
> "Shall I who cause delivery shut up the womb?"
> says your God.

And it shall happen SWIFTLY—right before the enemy. Every plot sought to abort the purpose, plan, and power of God will be destroyed, and when God delivers you, everyone will know it. You will see deliverance in your life, and so will the enemies of God. The fruit of your life will give witness when you least expect it.

Don't miss the future by trying to gauge how exactly God has done it in the past. Neither you nor I can predict the gestational period or the method of delivery for what God will birth in our lives. Not one of us can judge or dictate the time or details of delivery to the Deliverer Himself. Let the Lord be glorified!!!! In the resounding deliverance, and in the birth of breakthrough, only God can bring forth swift transition and delivery that baffles and boggles minds.

Before the arduous labor, know that it's already done. Before the pain comes, know that the favored blessing shall appear. This awesome foretelling for the people of God speaks a promise to us even today. It speaks of hope for faithful believers everywhere in the struggle. Remember: the promise will come forth quickly, after the season of preparation.

PRAYER:

**Father, we anticipate You! We celebrate,
in advance, that our preparation is not in vain.
Fulfill every promise to advance Your kingdom.
Heal hearts. Restore shattered lives.
Transform us and be provision, through us,
while we wait.**

Christ's Love Speaks Through Our Lives

JOHN 13:34-35 NKJV
A new commandment I give to you,
that you love one another;
as I have loved you, that you also love one another.
By this all will know that you are My disciples,
if you have love for one another.

In other words,
The world will know that we belong to Him
by the way we treat others.

Love is shown through our grace and benevolent service to one another. Those who consider themselves a part of God's family have a responsibility — not only to God — but to graciously journeying with one another in love, bearing one another's burdens. We share love through kindness, honoring each other as Divine image bearers, sharing time, talents and resources to help meet practical needs, prayer and encouragement, learning, growing and serving together. Christ's love through us sometimes looks like hospitality to our neighbors. Yet, to those we deem as hard to love, love seeks the betterment of all individuals, no matter their response. The truth is that Christ expressed that our love for one another will reveal Him to others. We love this way by the Holy Spirit's presence and power within our hearts.

Love is a word that is often overused but not always fully expressed. 1 John 4:17-19 says that perfect love casts out fear and empowers one to stand. We are Christ's disciples—children of God. Let us be courageous enough to live loudly by loving boldly because of the inexhaustible, inexplicable, and everlasting love of the Father. God is the Father who cannot forget us, just like a mother cannot forget the babe nursing in her bosom. God loved us first, and we will never fully live until—by His grace—we learn to truly love with hearts of gratitude for the greatest love we have received. Let your life speak by allowing Christ's love to flow through you.

PRAYER:

**Abba, each day, help us to embrace and fully walk in the softness and strength that is an intricate part of our way of being.
Soften our hearts that we may see others through Your eyes and not through the hidden lens of our woundedness, our troublesome past, or our self-dividing walls.
Though we have barriers and defense mechanisms, these fortresses fail to protect us.
Like privatized prisons,
they only erect monuments to misery which keep us stuck in the same place.
Heavenly Father, we surrender.
Let Your love flow through us
so we can let our lives speak of You.**

Come Out

1 Samuel 10:21-23 KJV
> *When he had caused the tribe of Benjamin to come near by their families, the family of Matri was taken, and Saul the son of Kish was taken: and when they sought him, he could not be found. Therefore they enquired of the LORD further, if the man should yet come thither. And the LORD answered, Behold, he hath hid himself among the stuff. And they ran and fetched him thence: and when he stood among the people, he was higher than any of the people from his shoulders and upward.*

The prophet Samuel had come, and the people wanted to choose and appoint a king that God would allow them to select. The tribe of Benjamin was called out, and Saul was chosen. Though Saul was being sought, he could not be found. Circumstances were not ideal because Israel wanted to be led by a king like the nations they observed around them, so God allowed them to have one. This was problematic because they chose to be ruled by man rather than be led by God. It is not a good thing to have the best and trade down because others settle for what is acceptable rather than seek what is best for them, but that is another story for another day. Samuel had previously anointed Saul. Saul of Kish, the tallest and most kingly in appearance, is revealed by God to be hidden among the baggage. Hidden and afraid, Saul was head and shoulders above the rest, yet he was shrinking back to avoid the call. Isn't that interesting? If we are not careful, we can find ourselves doing the same. We could be called out but can lead a life where we hide ourselves, just like Saul. In case you think this is the best route, let me remind us:

- Π Baggage cannot conceal what God wants to reveal. Saul steeped himself in the baggage. What were likely baskets meant to carry something useful and take things from one place to another are exactly what Saul chose to cover himself with, in cowardice. What would have served well to carry something became both a barrier and blockage. In the end, we see that it is God who reveals and uncovers Saul.
- Π What God reveals, God can heal.
  It is unfortunate that Saul's behavior was a pattern he refused to let go of. He hid behind insecurities and fears instead of allowing God to reveal and heal. Eventually, it cost him much more than he thought it could have.
- Π Know when it's time to come out.
  God gave away the hiding place of Saul because it was time to come out. Yes, there is a moment when it is time to come out from the baggage.
- Π Unpack the suitcase.
  This requires God's revelation, discerning strategy, and willingness to sacrifice, but it is worth the effort and the reward for all who are

appointed and anointed to be useful in God's hands.

II Promotion can be tied to commotion.
As we can see here, does not always come through ideal circumstances. Allow God to use you anyway.

God is uncovering what is hidden. You must come out so God can use you to lead and to serve others for greater impact and for God's glory.

PRAYER:

**Lord God, by Your discerning Spirit,
help us come out of hiding to occupy the space
ordained for us in every season, for Your glory.**

About the Author

Dr. Latisha D. Reeves Henry, a former teen mother at age 14, has been a long-time advocate of empowering others. She has been afforded the opportunity to travel to several other countries to speak and facilitate workshops in Burkina Faso and Nigeria in West Africa, Wiespden, Germany, and Kenya in East Africa. She served as the keynote speaker for Knoxville's annual TTOPS Conference for teen parents sponsored by the Knox County Health Department. Dr. Henry was the first female licensed and ordained to preach and serve as pastor in the 100+ year history of the Mt. Olive Baptist Church in Knoxville, TN.

Latisha is a member of Delta Sigma Theta Sorority, Inc. and has an amazing daughter who is a graduate of the University of Louisville. She is the founder of Dare2B U and author of Dare to Be You: Phenomenal Evolution. Dr. Reeves Henry has also been a contributor to a women's writing collective. She is married to the love of her life, Dr. Avery C. Henry.

Connect

www.daring2b.org
www.facebook.com/Dare2BUInc/
www.instagram.com/udare2b

Podcast: Daring 2 B U
Send book praise and reading group pictures to:
iam@daring2b.org